General editor
EVANGELIA KYPRAIOU

Proof reading
LITSA KATSA
VASSILIKI KREVVATA

Artistic supervision
VANA MARI

Translation
DAVID HARDY

Photographs
Archaeological Receipts Fund Photographic Archive: Figs 5-7, 11-14, 16-17, 20, 25-26, 63-64, 66, 69, 79, 95-96, 98-101 (photographer: Ilias Georgouleas); figs 23-24, 27-42, 45-62, 65, 67-68, 70-78, 80-94, 97 (photographer: Velissarios Voutsas).
German Archaeological Institute Photographic Archive: Figs 2, 4, 8, 21.
The engraving in fig. 1 was photographed in the Gennadeios Library (photographer: Ilias Georgouleas).
Ph. Zapheiroupoulou Photographic Archive: Fig. 15.

Cartography
KATERINA VLACHOU

Typesetting
S. KOSTARA
ARGYRIS VAVOURIS

Photo reproductions
P. ANAGNOSTOU

Printing
EPIKOINONIA LTD

© 1998
Archaeological Receipts Fund
Direction of Publications
Panepistimiou 57, Athens 105 64

ISBN 960-214-902-7

MINISTRY OF CULTURE
ARCHAEOLOGICAL RECEIPTS FUND

PAROS

PHOTEINI ZAPHEIROPOULOU
Honorary Ephor of Antiquities

ATHENS 1998

Like the marble of thy land,
brilliant and hard, no ferryman
shall destroy thy glory, Archilochos,
that stands erect side by side with Homer.

KOSTIS PALAMAS
Satirical Exercises, First Series

PAROS

Paros, the third largest island in the Cyclades after Naxos and Andros, is surrounded by the following islands: Mykonos, Delos and Tinos to the north, Syros and Siphnos to the west, and Ios and Iraklia to the south. Together with Antiparos and Despotiko to the west, it forms the Province of Paros. It and the neighbouring island of Naxos have been two of the most important islands in the Cyclades from ancient times to the present day. Its growth and prosperity throughout the centuries have been owed in large measure to its vital geographic position in the central Aegean, on the commercial sea routes linking mainland Greece with the Greeks of the eastern islands and the Asia Minor coast, and the coasts of the Mediterranean in general.

Amongst the distinctive features of Paros are the soft outlines of the island and its predominantly tranquil landscape. The great archaeologist Chr. Karouzos described Paros as "roughly a triangle on the sea, a simple shape: its sides however, curving here, bending slightly there, do not allow it the purity and coolness of *forme pure*, but rather give it something of the warmth of life".

The mountain range of Marpissa rises in roughly the middle of the island, the highest peak in it, Prophitis Ilias, being a mere 706 m. From this range start a number of heights descend gently to the sea, with plains between them, except on the north-west coast, which is fairly steep. Three deep bays on the north (Naoussa), west (Parikia) and east (Marmara) offer a pro-

Fig. 1. Old map of Paros and Antiparos. From O. Dapper, "DESCRIPTION DES ISLES DE L'ARCHIPEL", Amsterdam 1703, p. 260. Gennadeios Library.

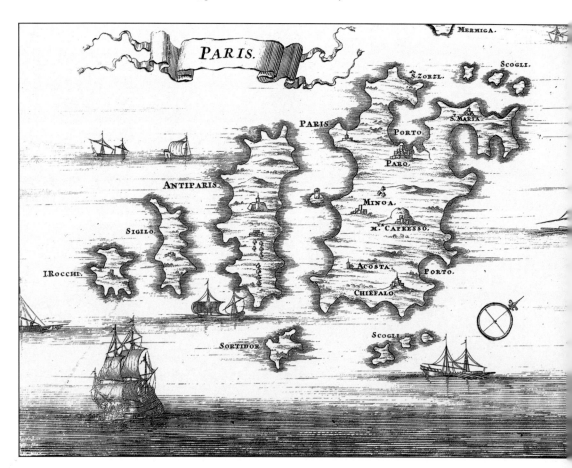

tected anchorage to seafarers in the normally rough seas of the Aegean. In the plains there are also springs of good, drinkable water. The rock of which the hills are formed consists of gneiss and granite, with strata of marble amongst them.

All these conditions were particularly favourable for human settlement, as early as the end of the fourth millennium BC, and on Saliagos, a small islet between the west coasts of Paros and Antiparos, traces of human occupation are attested even earlier, from the end of the fifth millennium BC. About 30 years ago, at the suggestion of the then Ephor of Antiquities N. Zapheiropoulos, English archaeologists led by C. Renfrew, uncovered a settlement dating from the Late Neolithic period (5400-4500 BC), which is one of the earliest in the Aegean. On Paros itself, the earliest traces of human habitation date from the period 3200-2300 BC, which is known as the Early Cycladic period, though very few settlements from this period have come to light. A large number of cemeteries have been excavated, in contrast, whose existence points to the presence of settlements. The best known early Cycladic sites on Paros have been located at Drios, Avyssos, Galana Gremna, Kampos and Plastiras.

In the following period, after the end of the Early Cycladic period, the first installations appear at Parikia (fig. 4), which is now the capital of the island. In the area of the Venetian castle, an important settlement was founded at the beginning of the second millen-

Fig. 2. Prehistoric settlement at Kastro. Early 2nd millennium BC (Phot. 1899).

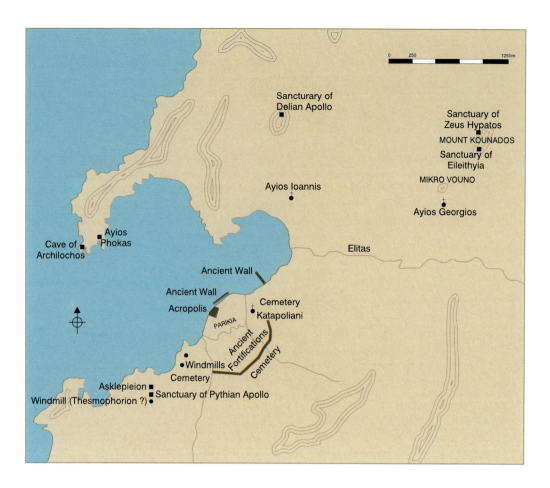

Fig. 3. Map of the area around Parikia (D. Berranger).

nium BC, the life of which continues into Mycenaean times and down to the Geometric period (1000-700 BC), as is clear from the excavations conducted at the end of the 19th and beginning of the 20th century by the German archaeologist O. Rubensohn and his colleagues (fig. 2). In the surrounding area of the city the German investigations also brought to light three sanctuaries, part of a Roman cemetery (belonging to the city) and the fortifications of ancient Paros (see p. 15).

At the north end of the island, on a rocky hill at Koukounaries (figs 5-6) on the north-west coast of the bay of Naoussa, the archaeologist's spade under the direction of D. Skilardi has over the last twenty years uncovered a second settlement, which prospered greatly in the Mycenaean period and particularly in the 13th c. BC. This settlement was destroyed about 1200 BC, but in the 10th c. BC, during the Geometric period, it was reoccupied and flourished once more in the 9th-8th c. BC, this period of prosperity lasting until about 650 BC.

During the course of the great migrations of the Ionian tribes, at the turn of the second to the first millennium BC, colonists from Attica came to Paros and chose to settle on the site of modern Parikia(fig. 3), near the sea rather than on a fortified hill, as was the common practice in the Aegean at that time. A factor contributing to this decision was the fact that there were already earlier settlements on this site. During the following, Archaic period, from 700-500 BC, Paros

Fig. 4. Parikia in 1899. View from the Delion.

experienced considerable growth and acquired power and wealth; it became a great cultural and commercial centre until almost the Roman period. Farming flourished thanks to the fertile plains, and the urban population worked in craft-industry activities. The main occupation of the Parians, was seafaring, and they even designed a new type of small, light ship, the *paron*. It is also indicative that one of the first figures to be depicted on the early Parian coins was that of the dolphin.

The economic growth of Paros, however, was due mainly to the founding of a colony on Thasos in the north Aegean, and the workings of the gold mines. The Parians settled on Thasos about 680 BC and the links between the mother city and the colony were not severed over the passage of the years. Working closely together with Miletos, Paros developed trading activities ranging from Egypt as far as the Propontis, where it took part in the foundation of Parion. In 385 BC, indeed, when the rest of Greece was in a not particularly creative phase, the Parians founded a new colony, Pharos, on a distant island off the Dalmatian coast, an event pointing to their enterprising spirit and energy.

Another source of the island's wealth was marble, which was amongst the best quality marble in Greece (figs 7, 8). One famous kind of white marble was *lychnites*; its name possibly derived from its lambency and translucency down to a depth of 3.5 mm, compared with the 2.5 mm translucency

Figs 5-6. Remains of the settlement at Koukounaries.

depth of the famous Carrara marble. Strabo tells us: "and so is the Parian stone, as it is called, in Paros, the best for sculpture in marble" (Strabo 10.5.7). To convey the whiteness of a marble stele, Pindar writes: "Set up a stele whiter than the stone of Paros" (Nemean Odes IV, 81).

In the 7th century BC rivalry with the neighbouring island of Naxos drew Paros into a series of wars from which she emerged defeated. One consequence of this was that the island ceased to be bellicose and began to practice a more pacific policy, so that it again acquired a relative independence and economic well-being. The number of free citizens in the 5th and 4th c. BC is reckoned to have been as high as 12,000. In the 5th c. BC. Herodotus (VIII, 112), states that the Athenian general Themistokles received "a large amount of money" from Paros in 480 BC. Another indication of the wealth of Paros is furnished by a historical event: in 489 BC the Athenian general Miltiades, the victor of Marathon, led an expedition against Paros with seventy ships. The outcome of the enterprise was not favourable for Miltiades, who, moreover, was wounded during the course of the siege. The official pretext for this campaign was that the Parians had Medised during the Persian Wars. It seems, however, that the Athenians were more interested in the riches of the Parians, in whose jurisdiction may have lain Eion, a city in the gold-bearing region of Mount Pangaion in East Macedonia, near the river Strymon. This

event is recorded by Herodotus (VI, 133): "Miltiades took his army and sailed for Paros, on the pretext that the Parians had brought this on themselves by first sending triremes with the Persian fleet to Marathon. Such was the pretext where of he spoke; but he had a grudge against the Parians because Lysagoras son of Tisias, a man of Parian descent, had made ill blood between him and Hydarnes the Persian. Having come to the place to which he sailed, Miltiades with his army drove the Parians within their walls and there besieged them; and sending in a herald he demanded a hundred talents, which (said he) if they would not give him, his army should not return before it had stormed their city".

At the beginning of the 5th c. BC, Paros began to lose its autonomy and was obliged to follow general historical and cultural developments, like the other Greek cities. After the Battle of Salamis (480 BC) the Athenians once more assumed leadership of the Greek cities and in 478 BC founded the first Athenian Confederacy, in which almost all the city-states of the Aegean took part. The Parians were also obliged to join and, as a wealthy city, Paros contributed more money than the other islands to the Confederate treasury. At the end of the Peloponnesian War, in 403 BC, Paros passed for a time under the control of the Spartans, but when the Athenians re-established their hegemony in the area, Paros became a member of the second Athenian Confederacy in 374 BC, which was dissolved in 338

BC, as the naval power of Athens waned and the leadership of the Greek cities passed to the Macedonians. At the instigation of Antigonos and his son Demetrios Poliorkitis, the Island League was founded with its religious centre on Delos; Paros was proclaimed free and autonomous. In 145 BC the island became subject to the Romans. The general decline observable in the archipelago during Late Antiquity, however, does not seem to have affected Paros, judging by a 5th c. AD inscription, which mentions the city on Paros, the asty, as "the most brilliant city of the Parians", which is probably no exaggeration.

For the larger part of the life of the city of Paros the political establishment was an oligarchy, though not in an extreme form, and as far as possible there was a relatively just distribution of social goods. The spread of the philosophical teaching of Pythagoras at the beginning of the 4th c. BC attests to the political spirit that prevailed. Pythagoras (580-500 BC) was a Samian philosopher and one of the founders of the science of mathematics. He founded a school at Kroton in Italy and several Parian philosophers and mathematicians are said to have studied at his School, including Thymaridas in the 6th c. BC, and Euephenos and Eukritos at the time of the foundation of the city of Pharos in the Adriatic, in 385/84 BC. In the 5th c. BC the activity is attested of an elegiac poet and sophist called Euenos, but the greatest intellectual and cultural figure not only of Paros but of early ancient Greek times, is the first lyric poet Archilochos, who wrote iambics and lived in the first half of the 7th c. BC. Son of Telesikles, a member of the upper class, and a slave called Enipo, he was an impulsive and stormy personality who led a troubled life. In modern terms, Archilochos might be called a "rebel". An inscription in the Museum (see p. 76) states that when he was still a boy, he was taking a cow to sell it in his father's instructions. It was dawn or possibly still night, since the moon was shining, when he met some women who joked with him and asked him to sell them the cow at a good price. They immediately vanished along with the cow, throwing a lyre at Archilochos' feet. When he recovered from his terror he realised that these were the Muses, who had given him the gift of a lyre, which accompanied him for the rest of his life. As the poet himself wrote: "I am the servant of *Enyalios* and know the desirable grace of the Muses". (Enyalios is an epithet of Ares, god of war.)

His father Telesikles was leader of a group of colonists that came to Thasos, at the beginning of the 7th c., possibly about 680 BC, an island with which they were bound by religious links: the father or grandfather of Telesikles, Tellis, together with the priestess Kleoboia, introduced the worship of Demeter to Thasos at the end of the 8th c. BC. The young Archilochos did not accompany his father on this colonisation venture but came to Thasos later, possibly as part of a second mission, having followed the example of his father and sought the advice of Pythian Apollo at Delphi. This must have been around 664 BC, when the poet was no longer in his first youth, but was about forty, and completely disenchanted with his life so far on Paros. On Thasos he fought in many battles between the colonists and the local inhabitants of the area, and tradition has it that he was killed during a battle between Thasians and Naxians.

In his work, which is unfortunately preserved only in fragments, Archilochos attempts for the first time to liberate the individual from the bonds of tradition and consciously to confront human insecurity in the face of the world and destiny. His personal answers

to these ethical problems are of assistance not only to the individual but also to society as a whole. Although his work frequently contains cynical barbs and is severely critical of his fellow countrymen, the Parians appreciated his great contribution and heroised him from as early as the Archaic period. The Archaic Archilocheion was possibly a cenotaph, though its form is not known; all that survives of it is an Ionic column capital (see p. 76). In the second half of the 4th c. BC a small prostyle Doric temple with two columns at the entrance was erected, enclosing the earlier capital. The Archilocheion was repaired by Mnesiepes after the middle of the 3rd c. BC, having received a command to do so from the Delphic oracle, and two centuries later Sosthenes, a descendant of the family

Fig. 7. Entrance to the Paros quarries.

Fig. 8. Votive relief depicting Pan and the Nymphs. From the quarry at Marathi. Hellenistic period (Phot. 1900).

of Mnesiepes again repaired the Archilocheion, though it was finally abandoned in the Roman period (fig. 9). In this small temple there will have been altars and probably also a statue of Archilochos, which may conceivably be the one depicted on two tetradrachms of the 2nd c. BC, on which he is depicted seated and playing a kithara. The precise site of the Archilocheion is not known, but it was probably built in the area of the river Elitas, not far from the city of Paros, on the road to the north-east.

It was not only letters that flourished on Paros from as early as the Geometric period, but also the arts: pottery and miniature art, executed in a variety of materials, mainly bronze. An important school of sculpture developed on the island in the second quarter of the 6th c. BC, thanks, of course, to the presence of the excellent marble, and Paros, which fell within the sphere of influence of Ionian art, developed into one of the largest and most important centres of sculpture in the ancient Greek world. Its creations were not only erected on Paros itself, but also travelled to many of the major sanctuaries from nearby Delos to distant Delphi. The sculptors themselves also travelled throughout the whole of the Greek world; amongst them was Skopas who, in the 4th century, worked not only in the Peloponnese, on the temple of Athena Alea at Tegea, but also in Asia Minor, on the temple of Artemis at Ephesos, and on the famous Mausoleum of Halikarnassus. Skopas is considered, quite properly, as one of the greatest sculptors of the ancient world. It was he who prepared the ground for the so-called Alexandrian baroque of Hellenistic art, by introducing violent movement in his figures, whose faces give expression to strong emotions. The names of several Parian sculptors of the 6th c. BC are recorded in a variety of ancient sources (written texts, inscriptions, etc): Aristion, Klenis, Kretonides and possibly also Charopinos and Arkesilas; several sculptors also lived and worked after the Archaic period: Euphron, Agorakritos (the favourite pupil of Pheidias, who worked with him on the Parthenon), Thrasymedes, and Skopas, just referred to above. Given this tradition, it was only natural that several innovations in the

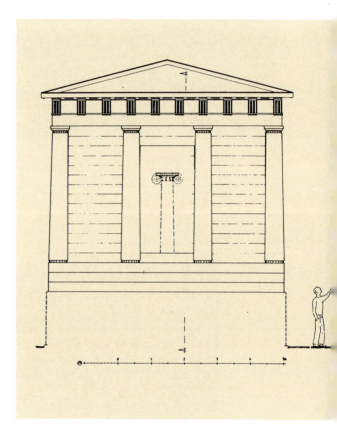

art were owed to Parian sculptors, amongst them the creation of the type of the grave relief, and also the type of the *kore* wearing an obliquely draped himation, which was more decorative and had a richer appearance than the hitherto known type, in which simpler garments were worn. With regard to the grave relief, the soil of Paros has lovingly preserved the earliest example so far known (see p. 59), (fig. 58).

The continuous occupation of the same area for centuries has meant that very few buildings are preserved of the important city of ancient times. As we have seen, Rubensohn was the first to establish the course of the fortification wall, which from the 6th c. BC on-

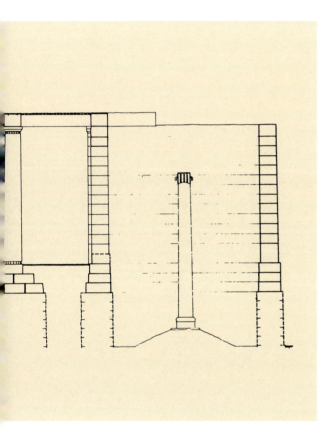

Fig. 9. Archilocheion. Reconstruction (AA 1982, p. 288, fig.11).

wards enclosed the city in a circle with a perimeter of 2.5 km. At the same time, four sanctuaries were also discovered, one of which was the main temple of the city. It stood on the hill of modern Kastro by the sea, was *hekatompedos* (that is, was one hundred feet, or 32.86 m, long), 16.50 m wide, and included a cella and pronaos; unfortu-

nately only the eastern part now survives, since the west subsided into the sea, together with the hill (fig. 10). On the east side it had six columns, and was therefore hexastyle, and may also have been amphiprostyle, that is, having columns on both the short sides. It was built about 525 BC and was dedicated to Athena, the patron goddess of the city. In addition to the foundations of the temple, a large number of architectural members have also been discovered, built into the circular Venetian (medieval) castle, in the construction of which use was made mainly of parts of the entablature of a rectangular stoa in the east Agora (figs 11, 12); this stoa was repaired at the time of Hadrian (second half of the 2nd c. AD). Members taken from a circular 4th c. BC structure which is believed to have been a temple of Hestia were used in the sanctuary apse of a small neighbouring church. Other public buildings mentioned in inscriptions, the *prytaneion*, *agoranomeion* and *demosion* (the State archive), have not been identified. The sites also remain unknown of the theatre and the temples of Dionysos and Kore (Persephone), whose temple was adorned with sculptures in the 4th c. BC.

For many years, A. Orlandos supervised restoration work on the famous early Byzantine church of the Katapoliani (see p. 24) (fig. 13), during the course of which much evidence came to light for the ancient city of Paros. Benches of an ancient theatre were found in the sanctuary, and mosaic floors from a gymnasium were uncovered beneath the floor.

At Tholos in roughly the centre of the ancient city, a public building of the Roman period was located some time ago, in which the famous Parian Chronicle was found (see p. 63). A Late Hellenistic house with a ground floor and upper floor was found nearby about thirty years ago by N.

Fig. 10. Temple of Athena at Kastro. Reconstruction of the west facade. About 525 BC. (AA 1982, p. 228, fig. 16).

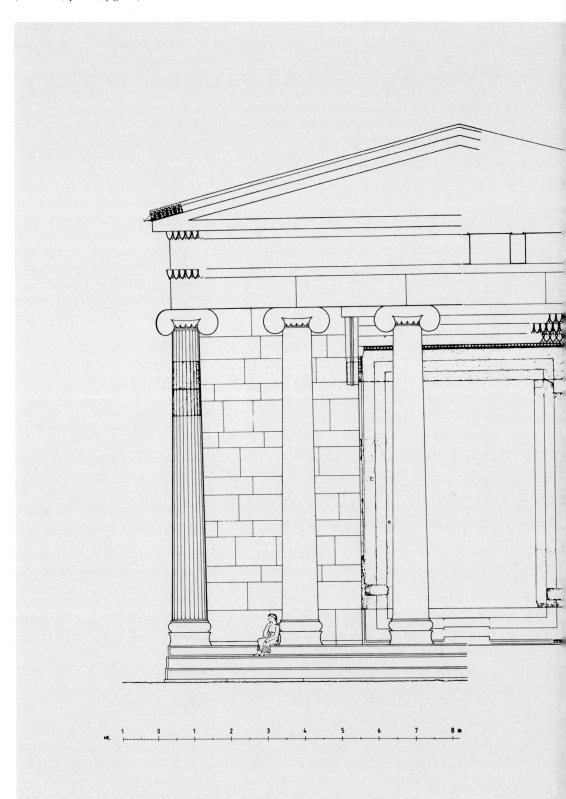

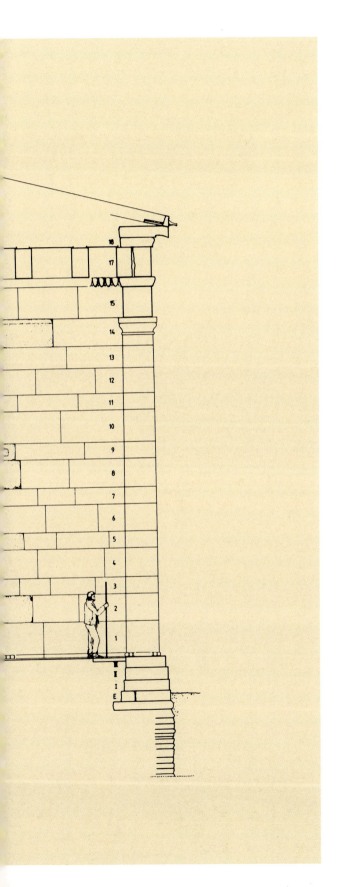

Zapheiropoulos, and recent excavations by the Archaeological Service in the same area have brought to light pottery (fig. 14) and sculpture workshops dating from the 4th c. BC or the Hellenistic period. Some meters away to the north-east, near the cemetery of Parikia, a Hellenistic villa with mosaic floors has been discovered. On the north-east of the city, close to the outside of the fortification walls, a large trapezoidal structure (?) has very recently come to light, though it is not clear whether this was an open or roofed one. It is too early to say what the function of this structure was, though it is not impossible that it was an enclosure with sacred character, judging by the equally recent discovery of a circular stepped monument with a lower diameter of 3.12 and upper diameter of 1.90 and a height of 1.50 m. Various drawings have been incised on the surface of the marble steps, including phallic symbols, soles of feet, etc. In the middle of top surface there is a depression to receive a statue or a stele. The relief slab A 1290 (see p. 50) was found to the east of this monument. The excavation of the area has not yet been completed, however, and it is possible that other moveable and architectural finds will come to light. This circular monument lies to the north-west and very close to the large trapezoidal structure which has dimensions of 26 x 15 x 20 m, and of which only the foundations survive; the initial phase of this structure apparently belongs to the Archaic period, though it continued in use down to Late Hellenistic and conceivably also Early Roman times. The kouros A 1282 and the statue base A 1281 were used as building material in one of these later phases, while the statues of a Gorgon (A 1285) and part of a torso (A 1284) (see p. 32, 47) were found fallen to the west of the structure.

A considerable quantity of architectural material from the

Fig. 11. Views of the castle; built into it are architectural members from the temple of Athena and a stoa in the east agora.

Fig. 12. Architectural members from the temple of Athena built into the medieval castle.

Fig. 13. The church of the Panayia Ekatondapyliani or Katapoliani. 6th c. AD.

numerous monuments that have not survived is preserved built into the modern houses of Parikia. This material has been the subject of study by German architects led by G. Gruben, who have been concerned over the last twenty-five years to produce a more or less accurate reconstruction of as many structures as possible, though naturally these have not been identified with specific architectural monuments.

At the city boundary, outside the walls and near the ancient harbour, a large cemetery has been discovered that was in use from the end of the 8th c. BC until about the 3rd c. AD (fig. 15). The site of this cemetery was noted thirty-five years ago by N. Zapheiropoulos, and at the beginning of the present century O. Rubensohn brought to light some marble sarcophagi from the Roman cemetery. This large cemetery contained burials of all kinds, and its use began at the end of the 8th c. BC with a group tomb or *polyandrion*, in which were about forty vases containing washed bones belonging to men aged between twenty-eight and thirty years. This *polyandrion* appears to have been the centre of a burial cult for at least two centuries.

Life in the city of Paros was not confined within the defence walls. Since the beginning of the 20th c. German excavations have brought to light sanctuaries on the surrounding hills: the sanctuary of Pythian Apollo and Asklepios to the south of the city, and that of Delian Apollo and Artemis to the north (fig. 3). The sanctuary of Pythian Apollo stood on a dressed level surface above the sanctuary of Asklepios and a few traces of its foundations can just be seen (fig.

Fig. 14. Pottery workshop. Archaic times down to the Hellenistic period.

16). The Asklepieion, at a lower level, covers an area of 45 x 15 m, near a source of water that has been in use down to the present day to supply the city's water needs. The water was required for the rituals carried out during the cult practised at the sanctuary. The Asklepieion included a rectangular building in the Doric order, which had stoas on the short sides (fig. 17); inside the building were long, narrow rooms, and at its centre stood an altar, surrounded by an open-air peristyle courtyard that linked the centre of the sanctuary with the sacred spring, near which there were two semi-circular exedrae. This sanctuary was built in the 4th c. BC, as, probably, was the sanctuary of Pythian Apollo. In a later phase, a few more rooms and a rectangular courtyard were added to the sanctuary of Asklepios.

Second in importance to the temple of Athena at Kastro, is the sanctuary to the north of the city on a high hill which has a view of Delos (fig. 20). This site was occupied by a prehistoric sanctuary, and about the 9th-8th c. BC, an area was created that was fenced around with an enclosure wall (dimensions 27.50 x 26.50 m) in which there was a small gate. Inside the enclosure a rock used as an altar for the cult of Apollo was surrounded by a pavement on which dances took place during the

Fig. 15. View of the cemetery at the city boundary, near the ancient harbour. 8th c. BC-3rd c. AD.

religious ceremonies.

In the early 5th c. BC, a marble temple dedicated to Artemis (dimensions 9.60 x 6.05 m) in the Doric order, with a pronaos and cella, was built in the north-west corner on the ruins of an earlier Archaic temple (fig. 19). An altar erected to the east of this temple was also erected dedicated to Apollo's sister Artemis (fig. 18), who was depicted in the colossal statue A 1251, dating from the 5th c. BC (see p. 78). In the 5th c. BC, various rooms were created to the south of the temple, including a banquet room (dimensions 4.70 x 5.30 m) with benches along the walls and an antechamber in front of it. The propylon of the sanctuary, of which the foundations are still preserved, was also built in the 5th c. BC. Behind the temple, at a slightly lower level, two steps led to a plateau with a panoramic view, where people waited for a light signal from the great sanctuary of Apollo on Delos in order to begin the festivities on Paros.

In addition to the above-mentioned sanctuaries, there were others throughout the entire Parian countryside: sanctuaries of Zeus, Hermes, Aphrodite, and above all of Demeter and Dionysos, two deities connected with the earth and fertility. In the low Kounados mountain range to the north of the road leading from Paros

Fig. 16. The sanctuary of Pythian Apollo, with the Asklepieion at bottom left.

Fig. 17. The Asklepieion.

to modern Naoussa, an inscription was found in a chapel of Prophitis Ilias that refers to the worship of Zeus Hypatos. To the west of the small church has been identified the cult of Eileithyia, the goddess who helped women in childbirth, and cuttings in the rock in the same area refer to offerings in a sanctuary of Aphrodite (fig. 21).

After 145 BC Paros was part of the Roman Empire. Judging by the sculpture workshops that functioned until about the 3rd c. AD (sarcophagi, grave reliefs, etc.) and even exported to other islands in the Aegean, the island continued to be artistically productive. In the following period, too, however, from the 4th c. AD, when Christianity became firmly established, down to the 6th c. AD, Paros seems not to have entered into decline; unless it enjoyed economic and therefore cultural prosperity, it is difficult to account for the erection of a monument as important from every point of view as the church of the Panayia Ekatondapyliani or Katapoliani, as it came to be known, which was built by Justinian (6th c. AD) at Parikia, on the ruins of a Roman gymnasium and an Early Christian 4th century basilica.

From the 7th c. onwards, however, Paros became prey to pirates, like other islands in the area, and was plundered, almost abandoned, and even became a base for the Arab (Saracen) pirates who polluted the Aegean for centuries.

In 1207, the Venetian M. Sanudo conquered the Cyclades and founded the duchy of the Aegean

Fig. 18. The altar of Artemis in the Delion. Reconstruction (AA 1982, p. 189).

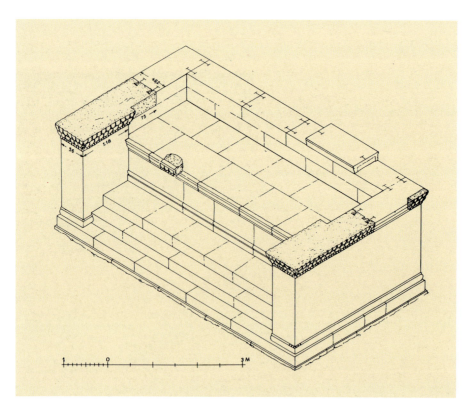

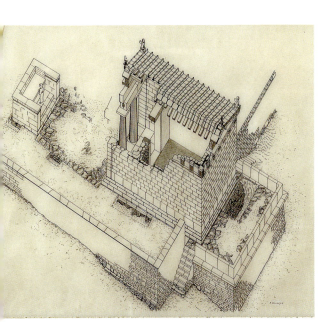

Fig. 19. The temple of Artemis in the Delion. Axonometric drawing (EAA IV, 1996, p. 261).

Fig. 20. The temple of Artemis in the Delion.

Fig. 21. Open-air sanctuary of Aphrodite on Mount Kounados (Phot. 1961).

with its seat on Naxos. In 1260 the Venetians built three castles on Paros, at Parikia, on the hill of the ancient acropolis where the already ruined temple of Athena stood, an area that is still today called Kastro, at Naoussa, in the north-east of the island, and at Kephalos, to the south of the bay of Marmara on the east coast, near modern Marpissa. All three castles are on coastal sites.

In 1389 Paros passed into the power of the Sommaripa family, a well-known ruling family in the Aegean. After this, it passed to the Venieri family in 1521, which was succeeded in 1536 by Bernardo Sagredo, who faced Haireddin Barbarossa in 1537 in a heroic defence of the castle at Kephalos, to which the seat of the administration had already been transferred by Nicolo Sommaripa (1462-1505). After the defeat of Sagredo the inhabitants were enslaved and despite the fact that the 18th century Aegean was a Venetian sphere of action, Paros remained under Turkish rule until the liberation of Greece from the Turkish yoke. It is stated, indicatively, that in 1675 Paros paid 6,000 piastres in tax to the Turks. During the period 1770-1771, the harbour of Naoussa was used as a base by the Russian admirals Orlov and Spyridov during the course of the first Russo-Turkish war.

THE MUSEUM

Fig. 22. Plan of the Museum.

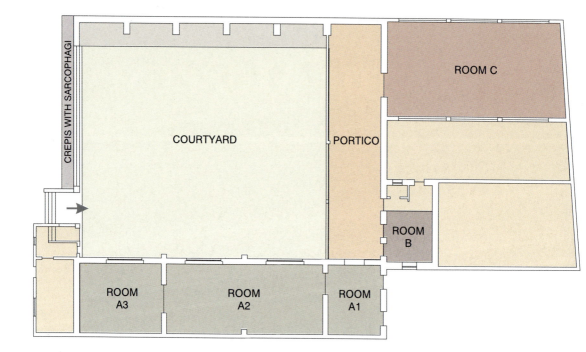

The first part of the museum building was erected in the 1950s. It was constructed as part of the High School complex, one long rectangular wing of which (figs 22, 23) was made available to house the antiquities, which until this time had been kept in the cells of the Church of the Katapoliani. The building was made over to the Archaeological Service in 1960 and the antiquities were transferred to it by the then Ephor of Antiquities N. Zapheiropoulos, who had just taken up his duties as Director of the Archaeological Service in the area. The exhibition of antiquities was designed on the basis of the objects that were already available, which were mainly 6th and 5th c. BC sculptures (fig. 23). At the same time endeavours were made to extend the Museum by the erection of a new wing (fig. 24, Room C), since the new excavations began to bring to light a large number of important antiquities, mainly sculptures. It should be added at this point that the Paros Museum is one of the few museums of ancient Greek art whose collections include original works of so-called grand sculpture, of the Archaic and Classical periods; this is of some importance, since our knowledge of the types, and the art more generally speaking, of Classical sculpture is based mainly on copies dating from late Hellenistic and Roman times, which make up the collections of the majority and the largest museums in the world.

The new wing (Room C) was handed over towards the end of

Fig. 23. The first part of the Museum building: Room A1-3. Display of sculptures dating from the 6th and 5th c. BC.

Fig. 24. The new wing of the Museum: Room C. Prehistoric, Classical, Late Hellenistic, and Roman objects.

Fig. 25. View of the Museum portico, with its display of sculptures and architectural members.

the 1960s, though it could not be connected with the previous building but formed a new, completely independent complex (fig. 22). The visit to this room begins with the prehistoric collection (to the left of the entrance), continues with later, Late Hellenistic and Roman objects (right side) and concludes with works of the 6th-5th c. BC, which could not be displayed anywhere else because of the shortage of space.

The two wings (A, C) are connected by a corridor taking the form of a portico, which in its original form was open along the entire west side so as to be communicate directly with the courtyard on its west. In a second phase, however, the north part of the west side of the corridor was closed by a wall that was deliberately kept low, so as not to create a completely closed area. In this "portico" were placed those of the sculptures that could be exhibited in a semi-open area that was not entirely exposed to the weather (fig. 25). The exhibition was later supplemented by new finds from the 1970s, including the colossal statue of Artemis from the Delion (see p. 78) and the 1980s. To the west this "portico" opens on to a large rectangular courtyard, which, like the ancient *atrium*, is enclosed on all four sides; on the north side there are rectangu-

Fig. 26. View of the Museum courtyard, devoted mainly to a display of funeral and votive monuments. In the background can be seen the church of the Katapoliani.

lar niches. In this courtyard an attempt was made, again by N. Zapheiropoulos, to exploit the Cycladic light in a composition involving ancient monuments and local vegetation, displaying all the brilliance of the Parian landscape with the dome of the Katapoliani in the background (fig. 26). The majority of the finds on display in the courtyard belong to the late artistic production of Paros and consist mainly of funerary monuments, with a smaller number of votives.

In the original form of the building there was a small office area in the east part of wing A. In the 1990s the office was transferred to a new structure that was erected near the entrance to the courtyard. The small room then became another exhibition area (B) which was designed in 1996 by our young colleague G. Kourayios, roughly along the lines set out by N. Zapheiropoulos. Room B contains mainly marble sculptures, with a few grave monuments and a larger number of votives, as well as a variety of small objects of Hellenistic and Roman date. Wing A also contains some important new finds of the 6th and 5th c. BC from the excavations at the ancient cemetery, in the open-air sanctuary (?) and in the surrounding area (see p. 17).

ROOM A1

The most imposing find in Room A1 is the statue of the Gorgon (A 1285) which welcomes visitors directly opposite the entrance (fig. 27). The figure is depicted descending from the heavens and landing on an antefix of Corinthian type. The statue probably crowned a votive (?) monument that was erected in a cult (?) area. According to legend, the Gorgon was a monster whose outward appearance was so terrifying that whoever looked upon it was turned to stone. The only depictions of it surviving from the ancient world, and especially from the early Archaic period, depict the Gorgon with the enormous teeth of a wild animal projecting from its mouth, snakes instead of hair on its head, etc. The Parian sculptor dispensed with all these external elements and attempted to convey the feeling of terror to the spectator in another fashion, by the size of the face and above all by its expression. The Gorgon is a young female figure, the upper part of whose body is covered by scales to suggest the fierce nature of the figure; the lower part of the body has gentle curves, with her garments "clinging" to her body as a result of her forward movement, while her enormous wings, stick "together", as they rise almost vertically above and backwards.

This humanisation of the Gorgon is not the only in-

Fig. 27. Statue of a Gorgon (A 1285). Probably the crowning member of a votive (?) monument. First quarter of the 6th c. BC.

novation to be noted in this outstanding work. There is a further point of originality in the naturalistic rendering of a running figure.

Down to the middle of the 6th c. BC, running figures were depicted with an angular, stylised movement of the lower part of the body in profile, on which sits the upper part, depicted frontally or, at best, turned three quarters to the side, as, in the so-called Nike of Archermos from Delos. With the ease deriving from his mastery of the art, the Parian artist portrays the figure in a normal running position; it is worked in depth with the whole body facing the direction in which it is running. In addition to the two innovations mentioned above, there is a third in this work: the capturing of the fleeting aspect of movement, an element so far known only from works in the following century, one of which is the Nike A 245 (see p. 50, fig. 46) the Gorgon dates from the first quarter of the 6th c. BC.

The Gorgon is surrounded in this room, or rather has recently been placed amongst, torsos of kouroi (A 165 lower part, middle of the 6th c. BC, A 167 upper part, about 490 BC) and korai (A 166, A 719, lower parts, second half of the 6th c. BC), which unfortunately retain little of their original brilliance. Nevertheless, in the places where the drapery or the modelling of the body have survived, one can still admire, even in their fragmentary condition, the Parian sculpture, which began to flourish as early as the second quarter of the 6th c. BC, the main feature of which are its soft outlines.

Kouroi are statues of naked standing youths normally with their left leg advanced in an attempt by the artist to give the figure movement; this is also the case with the korai, young clothed women, whose dress becomes richer towards the end of the 6th c. BC.

Other items on display in this room

Fig. 28. Grave stele with a depiction of a female figure (A 1287). About 480 BC.

include: at the back left, a relief of the late 6th c. BC with a seated figure of a bearded man (A 1177), which was dedicated in a sanctuary on Kounados, an open-air mountain area to the north-east of Parikia; at the top right of the wall is a shelf containing part of an egg-and-dart moulding (A 848) and to the right of the entrance, lower down, are grave stelai (A 169, A 769, A 182) and above them inscriptions of the Archaic period (A 58, A 766, A 767). Near the right jamb of the entrance to the main room (A2), a small stele of a young female figure (A 1287) (fig. 28), of which unfortunately only the lower part of the body from the waist down is preserved, expresses all the charm of Parian art about 480 BC. The body of the young girl, full of youthful vigour and suppleness, with its gentle curves, is outlined gently below the delicate, richly folded garment, the strongly sculptured quality of which gives rise to a chiaroscuro effect.

Fig. 29. The lower part of a colossal statue of Athena Promachos (A 91 and A 800). 480-470 BC.

Fig. 30. Colossal statue of a seated goddess (Artemis?) (A 162). Early 5th c. BC.

ROOM A2

Just to the right of the entrance to Room A2, before the window, is displayed a superb Protoionic capital dating from the 6th c. BC (A 929), above which, on a shelf, is a corner of an Ionic moulding (A 590), also of the 6th c. BC.

On the left side of room A2, visitors stand in awe before two colossal statues: one of them, A 91 and A 800 (mended from a large number of fragments) preserves the lower part, from the top of the shins down, of a female figure striding vigorously to the right (fig. 29). The left leg is advanced, with the full sole standing on the plinth. The figure wears a "Laconian" peplos that covers the legs down to just above the ankles and falls in a series of distinct waves as a result of the vigorous movement of the figure. The legs are unfinished. This is a monumental rendering of Athena Promachos in battle, dating from the beginning of the Severe Style, 480-470 BC. The second colossal work is the statue of a seated goddess (A 162), height 1.57m, mended and restored in places (fig. 30). It was found in pieces in south-east Paros, in the "field of the Dragon", in the interior of the island. The goddess wears a heavy, draped chiton and obliquely worn himation, and sits on a throne with a backrest and Aeolic capitals on the two armrests at either side of the front. The figure rests her legs on a footstool, is seated on a cushion, and apparently had her two arms held out in front of her; in the right hand she possibly held the symbol of her divinity. Missing parts include the head, the arms and parts of the throne. This is a work of the late Archaic period, probably from the beginning of the 5th c. BC, and was most probably a cult statue of Artemis.

Directly opposite the enthroned goddess, to the left of the entrance to the room, is a large relief slab (A 759) with a scene of a bull being torn apart by a carnivore (probably a panther in this case) (fig. 31). This slab, and another like it (A 758) (fig. 32), which is displayed behind the partition at the back of the seated goddess, were found during the restoration work on the church of the Katapoliani. The two slabs probably come from the so-called Archilocheion, a monument dedicated to the great creator of lyrical satiric poetry, Archilochos (see p. 13).

These slabs are thought to have surrounded the pit in which sacrifices will have been made in honour of the hero, though it is not impossible that they belonged to the late Archaic heroon itself, the form of which is not known. They are dated around 500 BC and it is highly likely that the second slab depicts Archilochos himself at a funeral banquet or a banquet scene in general. The poet is shown at the centre of the scene on the couch, his wife (?) seated at the left, a slave at the right, and in the background are items of military equipment (breastplate, shield, etc.) and also a lyre. The table that will have been depicted in front of the couch was probably made of

Fig. 31. Relief slab with a scene of a panther (?) pulling down a bull (A 759). About 500 BC.

Fig. 32. Relief slab probably depicting Archilochos at a funeral banquet or symposium (A 758). About 500 BC.

metal or had metal decoration. Two other important objects in this room take us to the 7th c. BC, the period at which Archilochos lived. These are two large vases (B 2652, B 2653), which in their first use may have served as grave markers, like modern crosses. They come from the large cemetery (see p. 20) and when they were found (see the drawing on the wall next to vase B 2652) they had been reused for burials of small children, and to this end the high conical foot had been cut away in order to release the fluids from the dead body. These vases are the product of 7th c. BC Parian workshops. One of them (B 2652) (fig. 33) with a mythological scene, and the other (B 2653) with a scene drawn from every-day life. The first vase has a scene set on Mount Ida near Troy, according to the legend, with the three goddesses Aphrodite, Hera and Athena (the names are mere conjecture, since the figures in this case have no particular distinguishing feature or symbol to identify them, as is usually the case in later depictions). The goddesses are being taken by Hermes to Paris, who welcomes them, in order to judge which is the fairest. His decision to give the prize, an apple, to Aphrodite, provoked the anger of Hera and thereafter the tragic fate both of Paris himself and of his native land, in the Trojan War. It is also worth noting that in this scene, the painter, probably out of a desire to allude to the natural environment in which according to the legend the scene took place, depicted four aquatic bird (ducks) behind Paris, one above the other, possibly in order to give a feeling of depth. On the belly of the second vase is a scene of a farmer cultivating the earth with a plough pulled by two oxen (see drawing on the wall), while the neck of this vase has a depiction of a hunter with a quiver and bow.

The Parian kouroi, which are now displayed in many Greek and foreign museums, with their solid but slender outlines and their body surfaces full of movement, are thought to be amongst the finest of the kind. On Paros one can also admire a number of examples which truly give expression to what the great scholar of Greek sculpture, E. Langlotz, inspired, has written to characterize the Parian Kouroi: "they breathe the dewy air of the mountain and the sea". The series of kouroi in the Museum has, in addition to the two in the previous room, four more in this room, giving some idea of the evolution of the kouros type during the second half of the 6th c. BC. Kouroi A 311 (at the right, near the first window), A 13 (fig. 34) (also on the right near the second window) and A 157 (fig. 35) (on the left opposite the stele of Archilochos) belong to the third quarter of the 6th c. BC and have slightly different dates. The fourth, A 1282, a recent find, is also the latest, being a work of the late 6th c. BC (fig. 36). As even the non-expert can see, the fluidity of the outline, the gentle volumes of the surfaces, and the strong differentiation between them, give this work a corporeality which make it a direct forerunner of the Severe Style that followed in the first half of the next century. This kouros may conceivably have stood on base A 1281, which has been placed next to it, as can be seen in the drawing in front of them (the two works, moreover,

Fig. 33. Large funeral vase from a Parian workshop, with a scene of the judgement of Paris (B 2652). 7th c. BC.

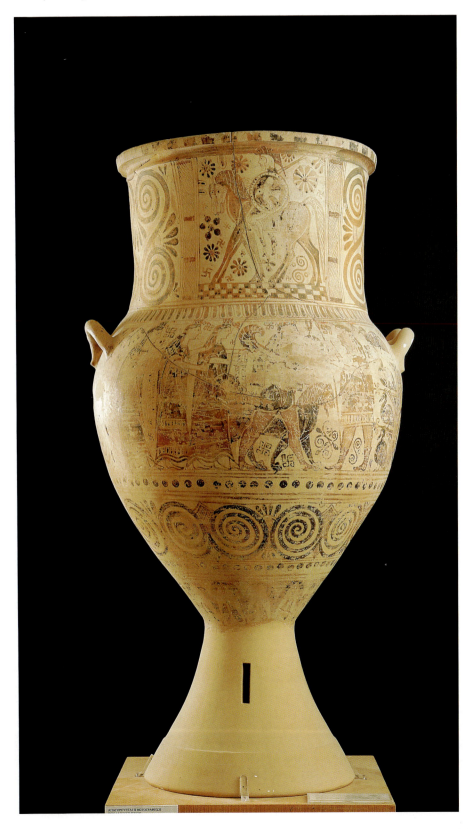

Fig. 34. Kouros statue (A 13). Third quarter of the 6th c. BC.

Fig. 35. Kouros statue (A 157). Third quarter of the 6th c. BC.

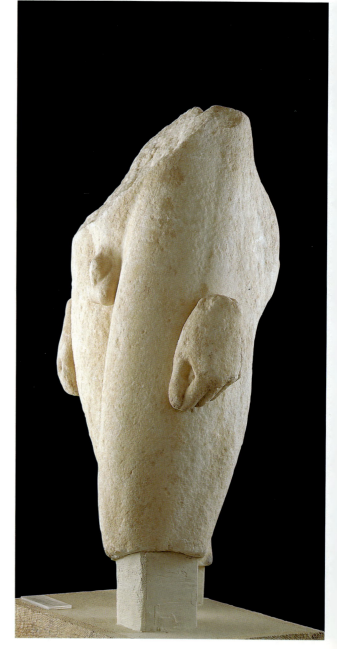

were found only 4 m apart).
The form of the base, at least as known today, is unique: on one side, probably the front, on which is the inscription ΧΕΙΟ (probably Chelon or Cheilon), it is an imitation of a column. The other sides are flat and end at the bottom in projecting semicircles that complete the circumference of the circle of the column base, probably for static reasons.

To the early 6th c. BC belong two very interesting reliefs that are illustrated in every handbook on Greek Archaic art. The votive relief A 244 depicts Hermes (at the right) and Artemis (at the left) moving towards each other, holding their symbols: Artemis the bow and Hermes the caduceus, the symbol of his capacity as messenger of the gods (fig. 38). One of the sides of this relief has an incised depiction of a palm tree. It dates from the end of the 7th c. BC. The relief A 172, at the back of the room on the right, depicts a Gorgon running

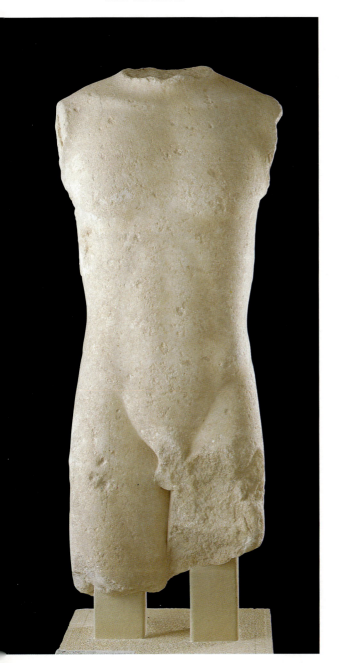

Fig. 36. Torso of a kouros statue (A 1282). Late 6th c. BC.

Fig. 37. Part of a statue of a male figure (A 1284). About 480 BC.

Fig. 38. Votive relief depicting Hermes with the caduceus and Artemis with her bow (A 244). Late 7th-early 6th c. BC.

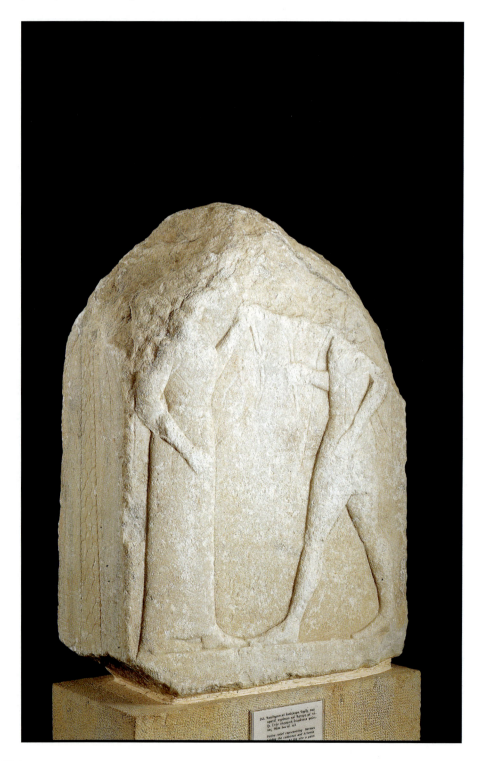

Fig. 39. Votive (?) relief depicting a Gorgon (A 172). Early (?) 6th c. BC.

Fig. 40. Marble palmette, the crowning member of a grave stele (A 119). About 480 BC.

Fig. 41. Part of a grave stele crowned with a palmette (A 1318). Middle of the 5th c. BC.

Fig. 42. Torso of a sphinx from the pedimental sculptures of the temple of Artemis in the Delion (A 194). Early 5th c. BC.

to the right with raised wings and her hands on her waist (fig. 39).

The other exhibits in the room are examples of the artistic output of the 5th c. BC. Impressive amongst them is the part of the torso of a male figure moving violently (A 1284) (fig. 37). The modelling of the volumes and the perfect finishing of the marble in a three-dimensional rendering of the figure find parallels in the famous bronze statue of Zeus from Artemision, now in the National Archaeological Museum in Athens. The Parian torso is a work of the Severe Style, dates from the third decade of the 5th c. BC. Another work from the first half of the 5th c. BC is a superb figure of an athlete painted on a marble disk (A 1168). He is a discus thrower who is depicted at the point when he is preparing to throw the discus. The figure is painted in red and his blond hair with gold, traces of which could still be distinguished when the piece was found. The discus that he will have been holding in his right hand may also have been painted in gold. The marble disk was found on the lid of a

Fig. 43. Parts of the large palmette that adorned the central akroterion of the temple of Artemis in the Delion.

Fig. 44. The temple of Artemis in the Delion. Reconstruction of the east facade (AA 1982, p. 242).

47

Fig. 45. Upper part of a torso of a hoplite (A 756) Second quarter of the 5th c. BC.

cinerary vase which will have contained the bones of a young athlete or man who was at some time a victor in the discus, and who was depicted at the moment of his victory.

The imposing palmette (A 119), on the wall at the left, was the crowning member of a stele; it is a fine example of decorative art in Parian grave stones, in which there is frequently an attempt to capture the majesty of the dead person (about 480 BC) (fig. 40). A smaller palmette (A 1318), at the right near the window, opposite the previous one (fig. 41) is considerably later in date. In the later palmette part of the stele is also preserved, and the volutes from which the palmette springs were probably painted. The freedom of outline in the leaves and their movement place the work in the middle of the 5th c. BC. Finally, on the left before the entrance to room A3, are displayed the few antiquities from the pedimental decoration of the facade of the temple of Artemis at the Delion, from the beginning of the 5th c. BC. The surviving pieces include the torso of a sphinx (A 194) (fig. 42) as well as the bottom (A 747) from the left side akroterion, and other parts of the fine large palmette (A 1356) on the central akroterion, as can be seen in the reconstruction drawing on the wall next to it (figs 43, 44).

Fig. 46. Statue of Nike wearing a peplos and sandals (A 245). From Parikia. Second quarter of the 5th c. BC.

Fig. 47. Upper part of a grave stele on which the head of a male figure is preserved (A 1026). About 440 BC.

ROOM A3

The next room, A3, contains works mainly from the 5th c. BC, the main exhibit being the famous Nike (A 245), a supreme work of Parian sculpture, and ancient Greek sculpture in general (fig. 46). It is a youthful female figure wearing a peplos open at the side and sandals on her feet. The head, wings and arms are missing. Nike was turning her head to the left, raising her left arm, while she held up the garment by the edge of the opening. Her right leg was suspended in the air, and she had just set her left foot on the ground. The speed of her movement has caused her peplos to open at the side, revealing her tender young flesh with its supple outlines; at the front the peplos clings to the body which can be seen beneath the thin material. The work dates from the second quarter of the 5th c. BC. This object dominates the room, but it is not the only one to depict a figure in movement. Another important sculpture is the torso of a hoplite (A 756) who is preparing attack, raising his right arm with the shield (fig. 45); this dates from the second quarter of the 5th c. BC, like the figure of Nike. Immediately to the left of the hoplite, is another statue in violent movement, again depicting a figure of Nike (A 183) running at full speed (fig. 48). This work is much later than the large figure of Nike (A 245) and dates from the end of the 5th c. BC; it is a typical example of the progress made in rendering a figure in motion in sculpture. The figure is depicted in flight and the diaphanous garment clings to her half-naked body blowing behind her in the wind. Unfortunately, in this case too, the wings, which will have strongly stressed the "flight" of the figure, are missing. Another relief, at the back right, next to the window (A 1290) is contemporary with this sculpture. It was found recently near a circular stepped monument (see p. 17), the function of which is still unknown. This relief depicts a young female figure with a thin peplos that will have had a metal belt beneath the overfall; she holds a circular object in each hand and walks to her left, thus giving the artist the chance to set the garments in motion, allowing them to blow in the wind, albeit only at the bottom.

Parts of three grave stelai in which

Fig. 48. Torso of a statue of Nike (A 183). Late 5th c. BC.

the heads of the figures are preserved give masterful expression to the Parian art of the relief, in which the alternation of light and shade plays a predominant role. The largest of them (A 1026), which is 2 m high and had a pedimental crown with antefixes, was the gravestone of a youth, the delicacy and nobility of whose figure, with its other-worldly gaze, profoundly move the spectator (fig. 47). It dates to about 440 BC (third quarter of the 5th c. BC), the period from which come two more young female figures on the small stelai on the right (A 1286) (fig. 49) and left walls (A 1093) (fig. 50); these stelai come from the large cemetery of the city near the harbour.

The display in this room is completed by the statue (A 757) from the sanctuary of Artemis at the Delion, devoted to the goddess by Arie daughter of Teisenor, according to the inscription in front of the figure's feet on the base. The goddess is rendered majestically wearing a polos (a high headdress), in a hieratic stance, and wearing a peplos with an overfall, while her hair hangs in long tresses down to her shoulders at the front and back (fig. 51). The piece dates to around 360 BC.

Fig. 49. Upper part of a grave stele that had a depiction of a young female figure, of which the head is preserved (A 1286). Third quarter of the 5th c. BC.

Fig. 50. Upper part of a grave stele crowned by a palmette, with a depiction of a young female figure, of which the head is preserved (A 1093). Third quarter of the 5th c. BC.

Fig. 51. Statue of the goddess Artemis in a hieratic pose, and wearing a polos (A 757). About 360 BC.

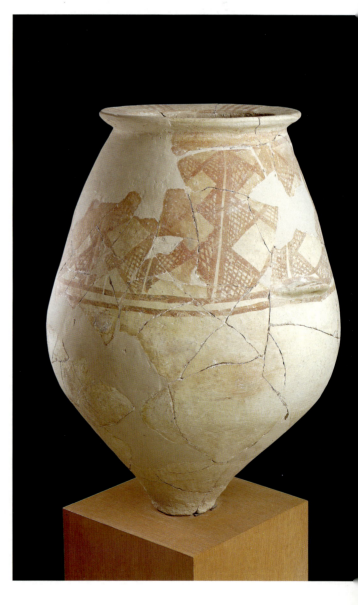

Fig. 52. Deep high-stemmed kylix with painted white decoration. From Saliagos. 4th millennium BC.

Fig. 53. Pithoid vase with painted geometric decoration, from the excavations at Kastro, Parikia. Second half of the 3rd millennium BC.

ROOM C

As we have already said, it is a good idea for visitors to proceed after room A to room C, in which objects are displayed in chronological order from the prehistoric period to late Roman times.

In case 1, at the left, are displayed finds from the prehistoric settlement on Saliagos dating from the Late Neolithic period (5300-4500 BC). Most of the items are fine clay vases with light coloured decoration on a dark surface (fig. 52), many of them resembling communion chalices (a unique shape in the Cyclades). One very fine object is the figurine depicting a female steatopygous figure, squatting, with her arms held below the breast. The case also contains a variety of stone tools, and blades and cores of obsidian from Melos, a very hard material from which were struck blades to be used as knives. The next case contains material from the excavations on the acropolis at Kastro with some fine painted pottery from the period 2300-1600 BC.

Between cases 1 and 2 is displayed a large pithoid vase with Geometric decoration, again from Kastro (fig. 53), as is a smaller vase on the other side of case 2. A shelf next to case 3 holds an enormous marble krateriskos (A 2200), a typical vase of the Early Cycladic period (fig. 54). This dates from the first half of the third millennium BC. The objects displayed in case 3 are also from the Early Cycladic period (3200-2400 BC). Almost all of them are grave offerings: on the top shelf are marble and clay krateriskoi; at the left of the middle shelf, a marble bowl preserves distinct traces of red paint (fig. 55); in front of it is a terracotta figurine depicting a pair of headless birds, just to the right of which are seashells, which are almost always found amongst Early Cycladic grave offerings; towards the right end of this shelf are pieces

Fig. 54. Small marble krater of the Early Cycladic period (A 2200). First half of the 3rd millennium BC.

Fig. 55. Marble bowl of the Early Cycladic period. First half of the 3rd millennium BC.

Fig. 56. Early Cycladic marble figurines of the Plastiras type. First half of the 3rd millennium BC.

of obsidian and bronze tools, while other larger stone tools are displayed on the bottom shelf. On the second shelf from the bottom is an interesting frying-pan vessel with incised decoration, the function of which is still unknown. It dates from the mature phase of the Early Cycladic period, roughly before the middle of the third millennium BC. At the right of the second shelf from the top there are a few marble figurines, one of the most characteristic objects of the Early Cycladic culture. Early Cycladic figurines are usually rendered with their arms folded below the breast and the soles of the feet sloping so that they do not rest on the ground. In contrast, the figurines here have the soles in the normal position. The earliest figurines of this type were found in the area of Plastiras, on the north coast of the Gulf of Naoussa (see map p. 90), after which these figurines are known as the Plastiras type (first half of the third millennium BC) (fig. 56).

Case 4 contains finds from the excavations at Koukounaries, the second major prehistoric site on Paros, which lies opposite Naxos. There was a flourishing Mycenaean settlement (13th-12th c. BC) on this site. Most of the objects are vases (the high-footed kylikes are characteristic) with painted deco-

Fig. 57. Part of a jar with a relief scene showing two figures fighting a duel. From Koukounaries. Second quarter of the 7th c. BC.

Fig. 58. Grave stele bearing the earliest example of a grave relief in ancient Greek art. It has a scene of a female figure seated on a throne. From the cemetery at Parikia. About 700 BC.

Fig. 59. Upper part of the torso of a kore statue (A 791). Found built into the medieval castle on Antiparos. Second half of the 6th c. BC.

Fig. 60. Torso of a kore statue (A 802). From the area of Naoussa. Second half of the 6th c. BC.

ration frequently inspired by the world of the sea, as in the large krater at the bottom right. Other objects of interest include the bronze vessels and tools, the sealstones and the bone artefacts. At Koukounaries, however, as we have seen (see p. 8) life continued after the Mycenaean period; in a building dating from the first half of the 7th c. BC was found a large part of a jar with a relief scene of two figures fighting a duel (second shelf from the top, centre) (fig. 57).

There follows a small suspended case containing sherds (fragments of pottery) from the city of Parikia and the countryside of Paros, covering the period from Mycenaean down to Classical times. The top shelf holds sherds of the 12th-10th c., the centre sherds from the 7th-6th and the bottom sherds from the 6th-5th c. BC. On the floor beneath the case stand large vases from the ancient cemetery near the harbour of Parikia.

In front of partition A, stands a large grave stele (A 760) which is the earliest example of a grave relief in ancient Greek art (fig. 58). It was found by N. Zapheiropoulos in 1960 in the area where the ancient 7th c. BC cemetery was discovered 23 years later. It depicts a female figure seated on a throne and turned to the right, worked in very low relief achieved by cutting away the surrounding area. In this way the artist attempted to liberate the figure from the flat background and incorporate it in space, giving it volume. The relief dates from about 700 BC.

Opposite partition A, in the centre of the room, two torsos of korai are displayed in front of partition B. Of the one on the left (A 802), which was found in the area of Naoussa, the torso and the legs down to roughly the knees are preserved (fig. 60). She wears a chiton which is girt around the waist and forms a kolpos. Between the folds of the lower part of the chiton are flat bands with incised maeander decoration. Of the second kore only the upper part of the headless torso is preserved (A 791) (fig. 59). It was built into the medieval castle on Antiparos. She wears a chiton in which vertical delicate undulating folds are worked by thickly set incisions. Both these works date from the second half of the 6th c. BC.

To the left of the korai and behind partition A, along the entire north side of the room, are showcases containing finds from the important sanctuary of Apollo Delios (see p. 21 f. and figs 60-66).

The top shelf of case 5 holds female figurines and fine female busts of the 6th c. BC (fig. 61), while the second shelf has Geometric figurines of the late 8th c. BC, and stone plaques with linear decoration; towards the right end of the shelf are displayed figurines of the 7th and 6th c. BC. On the third shelf from the top, and at the front left are figurines and objects imported from Egypt, amongst them scarabs made of faience, in the centre are displayed fibulae made of bone and a variety of small objects (fig. 62): amulets, earrings, finger-rings, seal-stones, etc., and below are blades and cores of obsidian, fragments of busts, beads and a bone flute in the middle at the front. The small suspended case next to it contains various types of terracotta Archaic figurines. On the bottom shelf are

Fig. 61. Terracotta heads of female figures from the sanctuary of Apollo in the Delion. 6th c. BC.

two figurines of seated female figures, and parts of large protomes with traces of red, white and blue paint. On the floor below the small suspended case is an inscription from the sanctuary of Delian Apollo which refers to Athena Kynthia (Kynthos is the sacred "mountain" on Delos).

The next case, no. 6, contains pottery from the sanctuary attesting to its relations with a number of important centres of the time, such as Corinth and the Aegean islands. The two top shelves hold Cycladic and Proto-Corinthian pottery of the 8th-7th c. BC (fig. 63), while on the other shelves are presented vases and fragments of vases from the 8th to the 6th c. BC, most of them from Cycladic workshops.

The following case, no. 7 also contains a large number of figurines, mainly heads of the 5th-

Fig. 62. Small objects made of bone: fibula, axe, and seal-stone from the sanctuary of Apollo in the Delion. 6th c. BC.

Fig. 63. Proto-Corinthian vases from the cemetery at Parikia. End of the 8th-middle of the 6th c. BC.

4th c. BC, on the top two shelves (fig. 64); the other two shelves also have many small objects dating from the 8th-4th c. BC, such as bronze fibulae and finger-rings (3rd, 2nd shelves). On the third shelf are terracotta animal figurines of a pig, a turtle, and birds, and in the front centre of the shelf a figurine of a dog, curled up. The same shelf has two small marble tables, one of which has three surviving legs which are in the form of a lion's paw. The tables date from the 4th c. BC. On the bottom shelf at the left are parts of female figurines of the 6th-5th c. BC, and at the right 8th c. BC beads made of glass paste; at the right end of this shelf is an item of importance, despite its fragmentary state of preservation: part of a votive relief dating from 480-470 BC depicting a male figure turning to the right. The figure is probably a musician, judging by the type of his dress: a long, broad chiton with simple drapery, characteristic of flute-and kithara-players. It was found in the Delion and it is not inconceivable that it depicts Apollo himself playing the kithara.

Towards the north end the east wall, three works of the Archaic period are displayed: an unfinished head of a kouros (A 792), a torso of a small kore wearing a chiton (A 163) and a fine head of a kore which may possibly have belonged to a statue of a sphinx (A 164). Beyond this are presented small-scale works of the 5th c. BC, many of them grave stelae. Important among them are the stelai A 947 and A 948. The former, which has a relief figure of a bearded man, is an outstanding work (fig. 68), akin to the figures on the Parthenon, many of which are known to have

Fig. 64. Terracotta heads of female and male figures from the sanctuary of Apollo in the Delion. 5th-4th c. BC.

Fig. 65. Geometric vase with painted decoration, from the Delion. 9th c. BC.

been worked by Parian artists; on the second stele is preserved part of a woman wearing a peplos, who was extending her arms in front of her and probably holding a band which will have been indicated in paint. It dates to around 440 BC. On stele A 783 are preserved the bottom parts of two figures walking towards each other, while on A 749 only the head survives of a young woman turned to the right; next to this stele is displayed a head (A 686) of a male statuette of 450 BC (fig. 67). Lower down on the wall are two inscriptions (A 780, A 156). To the right, on the south wall, three more objects: a headless enthroned female figure (A 19) wearing a peplos belted beneath the breast and a himation, another headless statue of a woman (A 459) with a chiton belted high and a himation (Athena?), and a relief (A 298) depicting a half-reclining woman.

Before continuing to the southeast corner of the room, visitors would do well to turn towards partition B. At the right is displayed the statue of a kore (only the lower part is preserved) running swiftly to the left (A 168). This may be a corner akroterion from a temple dating from the last quarter of the 5th c. BC. At the spectator's left end of this side of the partition is an inscribed slab which is one of the most important monuments of the ancient Greek world. It is part of the so-called Parian Chronicle (fig. 69); the story of its discovery and subsequent adventures begins in the 17th c., when two of the three parts of an inscribed stele of white marble were found, probably in Kastro at Parikia, and taken to Smyrna by an

Fig. 66. Two small marble tables from the sanctuary of Apollo in the Delion. 4th c.BC.

Fig. 67. Head of a statuette of a male figure (A 686). 450 BC.

antiquities-dealer named Sampson. There he was arrested by the Turks and in 1627 this collection of antiquities was bought by an English agent on behalf of the Earl of Arundel, whose nephew, in 1667, presented two sections of the stele to the University of Oxford, where they have been kept down to the present day. About 250 years later, in 1897, the third part of the stele, containing 32 lines, was found in the region of Tholos at Parikia, and is now housed in the Paros Museum (A 26). This inscription, which is widely known as the Parian Chronicle, contains 134 lines giving a chronological table of the birth or death of the most important intellectuals of the ancient Greek world (Greece and the colonies) and also important events, such as Xerxes' campaign against Greece, the occurrence of natural phenomena, etc. This chronological table covers a period of 1318 years, from the time of Kekrops, the first king of Athens (1582 BC), to the period of the Athenian archon Diognetos (264/263 BC). Curiously, there is no mention of Parian history and no information relating to events connected with Paros or the Cyclades. The references on the stele are to events of pan-Hellenic importance and according to one theory the stele may conceivably have been erected in the area of the sanctuary of Archilochos (see p. 13 f.) to be read, possibly as part of a history lesson, since the Archilocheion contained a Gymnasium, that is a place of public education. The stele was inscribed in the middle of the 3rd c. BC by some Parian man

Fig. 68. Part of a grave stele with a figure of a bearded man (A 947). 5th c. BC.

Fig. 69. Inscribed slab, one of three parts of the stele on which the Parian Chronicle is inscribed (A 26). Middle of the 3rd c. BC.

Fig. 70. Parts of a sima with palmettes (A 442). Found built into the church of the Katapoliani. 4th or 3rd c. BC.

of letters, who has remained unknown to the present day.

Returning to the south part of the room, visitors may see on the upper part of the east wall three parts of a fine sima with palmettes dating from the 4th or 3rd c. BC (A 442) (fig. 70), and lower down, from the left: a 4th c. BC torso of a statuette of Artemis (A 23), wearing a peplos girt below the breast and depicted in vigorous movement, with her left leg advanced and her left arm raised, the upper part of a small pillar with a female head (A 376), and two male heads, one of Asklepios, found in recent years in the pottery workshop (see p. 17) and one of Dionysos (A 171) with an ivy wreath.

In the south-east corner is a stepped structure on which are displayed marble slabs with relief depictions of legs and arms, which were dedicated to Asklepios, the god of medicine (A 183, A 184, A 187, A 188 (fig. 71), A 937, A 99)

Fig. 71. Votive slab carved with relief hands, dedicated to Asklepios (A 188). Hellenistic period (?).

or to Eileithyia, the goddess of childbirth. These dedications are like the modern *ex votos* in churches representing the limb that needs to be healed or that has already been healed. Behind these at the beginning of the south wall is a relief with five figures (A 32), three of them adults: at the left is a man wearing a himation and two women in the type of the small Herculaneum woman familiar in the Hellenistic period; at the feet of these figures to the right and left are two children. Next to them is displayed a statuette probably of Aphrodite (A 25), and further to the right a small pediment (A 107) with a depiction of a gorgoneion on the tympanum, which probably comes from the upper edge of the side of an altar (4th c. BC).

The next case, no. 8, has a display of objects from Parikia and the surrounding area which date from the late 6th c. BC down to the 2nd c. AD, most of them from the cemetery near the ancient harbour (see p. 20). On the top shelf are displayed mainly Attic pottery, amongst which are a number of black-figure (end of the 6th c. BC) and red-figure (5th c. BC) vases, largely at the right end of the shelf. On the second shelf down are an assortment of glass vases of Roman times (1st-2nd c. AD) (fig. 73), while the third shelf holds pottery and terracotta figurines of the 5th-4th c. BC. Amongst the latter there is an interesting dolphin with a little girl on its back (fig. 72), and three lozenge-shaped pieces of marble from children's tombs which were used as toys, as can be seen in the drawing next to them (fig. 74). At the back left is a lantern used to carry a lighted lamp, which was discovered in a child's tomb. At the right, terracotta figurines of Hellenistic and Roman times. On the bottom shelf are a variety of small objects: bronzes, mirrors and strigils (in-

Fig. 72. Terracotta figurine of a dolphin with a girl sitting on its back. From a tomb in the ancient cemetery. 5th-4th c. BC.

Fig. 73. Glass vases of Roman date from tombs at Parikia. 1st-2nd c. AD.

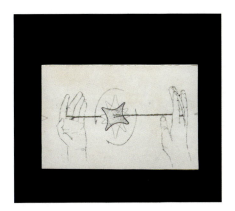 

Fig. 74. Three lozenge-shaped pieces of marble, which were used as a child's toy, as shown in the drawing. From child tombs in the cemetery near the ancient harbour. 5th c. BC.

struments used by athletes to cleanse their body of oil and sweat after the end of training), bone objects, gold jewellery (fig. 75), finger-rings, pins, etc.

After this, at the right side of case 8, are displayed grave reliefs and a few sculptures dating from the 4th c. BC down to the end of the Hellenistic period: a grave stele in the shape of a temple with a pediment and akroteria (A 734), on which are portrayed two figures, a seated male at the left with a standing female in front of him, in the commonly found scene of farewell in which people bid farewell to the dead person, usually the seated figure (fig. 76). There follows a bipartite base (A 363) from another grave stele bearing the name of the dead person, and above it, on the wall, the front part of a small statue of a lion turning its head to the left (A 990). In front of this and to the right stands the statue of a kore with a chiton and himation, holding a hare to her breast (A 461), and just behind this is displayed the lower part of an inscribed grave stele on which a hoplite is depicted standing with his legs astride on the prow of a ship (A 1). High up on the wall is part of grave stele with floral decoration (A 365). Opposite this group of reliefs, in the space between them and partition B with the Parian displayed two reliefs are displayed either side of a small partition: a votive relief (A 256) facing the east side of the room, on which is depicted a woman with a quiver and two torches, lighting a fire on an altar (fig. 78), and a relief with a horseman (A 794), which faces the centre of the room.

The visit to the museum continues with the south wall, where there is a series of grave reliefs: A 369 with a seated man and a standing woman, A 295 with a seated woman stretching out her hand to take a small box offered to her by a young girl, and A 170 with painted decoration of an Ionic moulding at the top and a Lesbian moulding at the bottom (traces of paint are still preserved) further to the right, part of the side of a sarcophagus with a

Fig. 75. Gold jewellery from the cemetery near the ancient harbour. 1st-2nd c. AD.

Fig. 76. Grave stele in the shape of a temple with a scene of farewell (A 734). Last third of the 2nd c. BC.

depiction of Eros running to the right (A 185). The other grave reliefs belong to the funeral banquet type A 180, A 796 (fig. 80), A 66, A 200, A 1214, A 181 (fig. 82): the dead person or persons recline on couches with a table in front of them, normally with three legs, bearing offerings. These reliefs frequently had vivid painted decoration, mainly in red, which is preserved in the case of reliefs A 1214 (fig. 82). Funeral banquets of this type are the work of Parian workshops of late Antiquity, in the 3rd c. AD. The funeral banquet A 181 (fig. 82) is in front of the partition C set at right angles to the wall, along with an unfinished male portrait head (A 782) (fig. 77) dating from the late Hellenistic period and another, male bearded figure, probably of Asklepios, dating from the 4th c. BC (A 345). Near the middle of the room are two cases (9 and 10) with finds from the large cemetery near the ancient harbour; on the bottom shelves of both

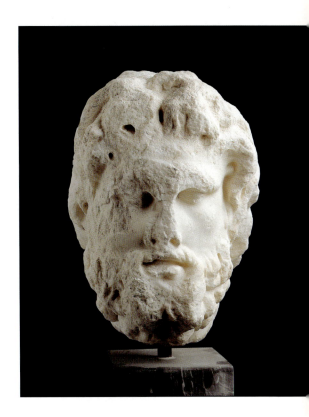

Fig. 77. Unfinished male portrait head (A 782). Late Hellenistic period.

Fig. 78. Votive relief with a scene of a female figure carrying a quiver and lighting a fire at an altar with two torches (A 256). 4th (?) c. BC.

cases are displayed Geometric vases of the late 8th c. BC (fig. 81) from the collective tomb, the *polyandrion* (see p. 20). On the top and third shelf of case 9 are some fine Corinthian vases of the 7th c. BC with a few terracotta figurines at the right of the third shelf.

The partition creates a fairly small area at the south-west end of the room which contains works dating from the 6th and early 5th c. BC. Two heads of male statuettes in the Severe Style (first half of the 5th c. BC): one is unfinished and comes from the Delion (A 223) and the other is from the Asklepieion (A 228) (Fig. 83). Next to them is the upper part of the torso of a kouros (A 898) and in the corner is a column (A 1321) which was reused as a kind of pilaster. An Archaic inscription in two lines is inscribed along the flutes, and at the top is preserved the name of a Parian artist of the first half of the 6th c. BC: ΠΑΙΣ ΗΟ ΗΣΕΝΕΔΟΚΟ ΠΟΛΥΑΡΗΤΟ Μ ΑΝΕΘΕΚΕΝ ΚΛΕ-

Fig. 79. Sherd from an open vase with painted decoration and a scene of a warrior. From the ancient cemetery at Parikia. 7th c. BC.

Fig. 80. Grave relief with a scene of a funeral banquet (A 796). 3rd c. AD.

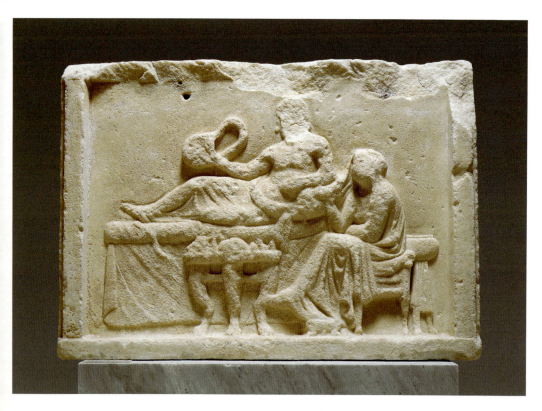

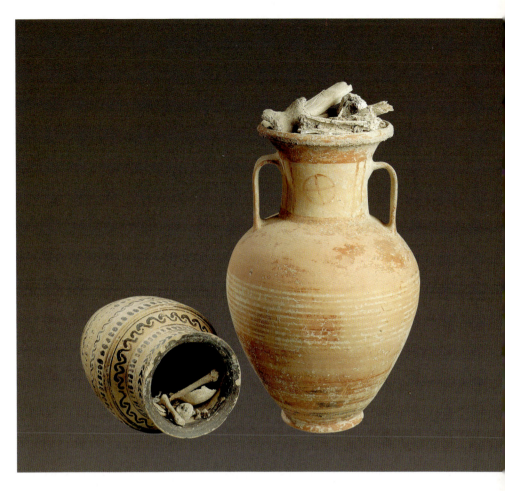

Fig. 81. Geometric vases from the group tomb or polyandrion. Late 8th c. BC.

Fig. 82. Grave relief with a scene of a funeral banquet (A 181). 3rd c. AD.

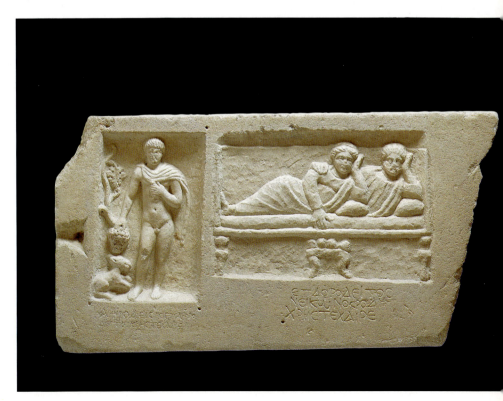

Fig. 83. Heads of male statuettes in the severe style: from the Asklepieion (A 228), left, and the Delion (A 223), right. First half of the 5th c. BC.

Fig. 84. Upper part of the torso of a kouros (A 249). 6th c. BC.

Fig. 85. Marble palmette, the crowning member of a grave stele (A 918). 470 BC.

Fig. 86. Grave relief with a scene of a funeral banquet, in which traces of red paint are preserved (A 1214). 3rd c. AD.

ΝΙΣ ΕΠΟΕΣΕΝ (Polyaretos, the son of Xenodokos dedicated me Klenis made [me]). The inscription refers to the dedication that will have been set on top of the column, which no longer survive with an Archaic inscription along the fluting. There follow a fine large palmette (A 918) dating from 470 BC, which is the crowning member of a grave stele (Fig. 85), and three kouroi, two of them (A 742 and A 285) with only the upper part of the torso and part of the upper arms surviving, while the (A 249) head of the third is also preserved with impressively rich hair (Fig. 84), though unfortunately the face is missing. On the west wall next to the entrance is a small grave relief (A 761) with its base and palmette crown (470-460 BC).

Fig. 87. Ionic capital from the Archaic Archilocheion (A 733). 6th c. BC. The inscription on the echinus dates from the 4th c. BC.

THE PORTICO

As visitors leave the room, the north part of the long portico opens before them to the right of the entrance; this area is devoted to Archilochos. In the centre is the Ionic capital dating from the 6th c. BC (A 733) (fig. 87), the only one preserved of the Archaic Archilocheion; an inscription was carved on the echinus in the 4th c. BC stating that this is the tomb of Archilochos, probably a cenotaph, erected by one Dokimos, son of Neokreon (see p. 13). In the middle of the top surface of this capital will have stood a statue, in all probability a sphinx, a subject of chthonic character commonly found in the crowning members of grave stelae. The drawings on the east wall of the portico suggest one hypothetical manner in which the Archaic column capital could have been set on the later Archilocheion, whose architectural form is also largely a matter of hypothesis. In the Museum display, the capital is supported by a modern column and surrounded by inscribed slabs, the texts on which refer to biographical details of Archilochos's life, and to events of his time (see p. 12 f.). Apart from stele A 92 (just to the right of the entrance), all the other inscriptions are incised on orthostates (architectural members), which probably come from repairs and rebuilding of the Archilocheion at different periods. The earliest inscriptions (A 176, A 177, A 175) date from the 3rd c. BC, when the monument was repaired by Mnesiepes (see p. 13), while A 40 (and possibly also A 732) are later by about 200 years, and date from the period when the monument was repaired by Sosthenes, a descendent of Mnesiepes. Inscriptions A 730 and A 731 are contemporary with it; in the latter (on the north wall) there is a relief depiction of the front part of a cow, which will have been a graphic depiction of the incident in which the cow was exchanged with the lyre when the poet met the Muses, as recorded in the inscription of Mnesiepes mentioned above. A 40 (near the north-west corner) was used in the 3rd c. AD as a grave monument, as is clear from the depiction of a funeral banquet on the rear. Of the inscriptions beyond this on the west wall, A 1080 includes a text in 90 lines relating to a proposal by a committee on the reform of the archive system on Paros, which was approved by the assembly of the people (second quarter of the 2nd c. BC). Of the following two large inscribed stelai, A 1076 contains a metric inscription consisting of nine elegiac distichs and A 179 has two decrees. Two slightly shorter inscriptions contain a list of the taxes paid for the grain-supply (A 36) and an honorific decree (A 29). Higher on the wall, above these two inscriptions, is displayed a large part of a sima (A 458, A 1351) with floral decoration and a lion's head in the place of the water-spout. This comes from the temple of Apollo built by the Athenians on Delos in the last quarter of the 5th c. BC.

In front of the inscriptions, at right angles to them and to the entrance to the room, is displayed a fine torso of a horse (A 778) dating from 490-480 BC, while a similar torso of a horse (A 1185), possibly a slightly earlier work, in which the head is also preserved (fig. 88), adorns the south part of the portico. Between the two horses

Fig. 88. Torso of a horse (A 1185). Early 5th c. BC.

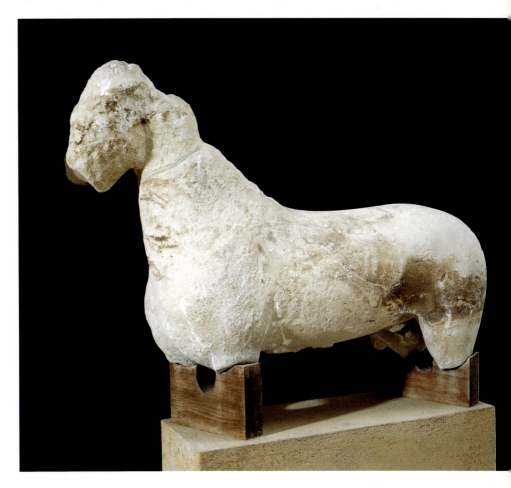

Fig. 89. Votive colonnette with the inscription ΔΙΟΣ ΕΛΑΣΤΕΡΟΥ (Zeus the avenger) (A 174). Used as a boundary marker in a precinct of the god. Middle of the 5th c. BC.

are an Archaic Ionic capital (A 775), probably from a votive column, like the ones dedicated by the Naxians at Delphi and on Delos, and a colossal statue of a female figure (A 1251), which comes from the sanctuary of Artemis at the Delion (see p. 22) and depicts the goddess with a chiton and an obliquely draped himation. The square base of the statue is also preserved and is displayed next to it. The statue and base are 3.70 m high. This was the cult statue of Artemis which stood in the cella of her temple at the Delion and dates from the decade 490-480 BC. It is one of the few examples of an original work on a colossal scale dating from the early 5th c. BC, created by the famous sculptors of Paros; despite its poor state of preservation, there is evidence at many points of the sculptural quality of the figure and the excellent workmanship. In this statue the artist has liberated the body from the Archaic *"rigidity"* and gives it depth, as he contributes to the creation of the Classical figure. On the south part of the east wall of the portico, just to the left of the entrance to the room, is a large corbel (A 1176) decorated with volutes, from a Classical building. To the south of it are architectural fragments (A 4, A 772, A 773) and below it parts of inscribed stelai (A 6, A 77, A 326); at the end is an altar support of the second half of the 5th c. BC decorated with volutes and palmettes. Beyond this are displayed other architectural members, one of which is decorated with a winding tendril and palmettes (A 845). There are also two sundials on the wall to the left of the entrance to room A: only part of one of these (A 1236) survives, while in the other the slab with the inscribed marks is preserved (A 865). Next to this, in the corner, is a votive colonnette (A 174) bearing the inscription *ΔΙΟΣ ΕΛΑΣΤΕΡΟΥ* (Zeus the avenger) (fig. 89). On the other side of the entrance to room A is part (A 1184) of a group depicting bull fighting a lion; the head of the bull and one leg of the lion resting on its head are preserved. Nearby is a fluted colonnette (A 1357) inscribed with the names of athletes (?). It possibly comes from the theatre of the city, and was later reused as part of a pilaster.

ROOM B

In the small room B, particular interest attaches to the suspended case to the left on the north wall; on the top shelf are terracotta figurines and casts, with small marble objects in the centre: a statuette (A 1229) of a kneeling woman wearing a himation (fig. 92), from the decoration on a sarcophagus lid, a statuette of a duck (A 232), a child's hand holding a dove (A 239), a hand holding a *rule*, (A 241), a hand holding an indiscernible object (A 215),

Fig. 90. Votive slabs from the sanctuary of Eileithyia. Top: (A 305) 2nd c. BC. Bottom: (A 306) 1st-2nd c. AD.

Fig. 91. Votive slab from the sanctuary of Eileithyia (A 307). 1st-2nd c. AD.

Fig. 92. Statuette of a kneeling female figure wearing a himation, from the sculptural decoration of a sarcophagus lid (A 1229). 2nd-3rd c. AD.

Fig. 93. Torso of a statue of a naked youth with a himation over his left shoulder (A 977). Hellenistic period (?).

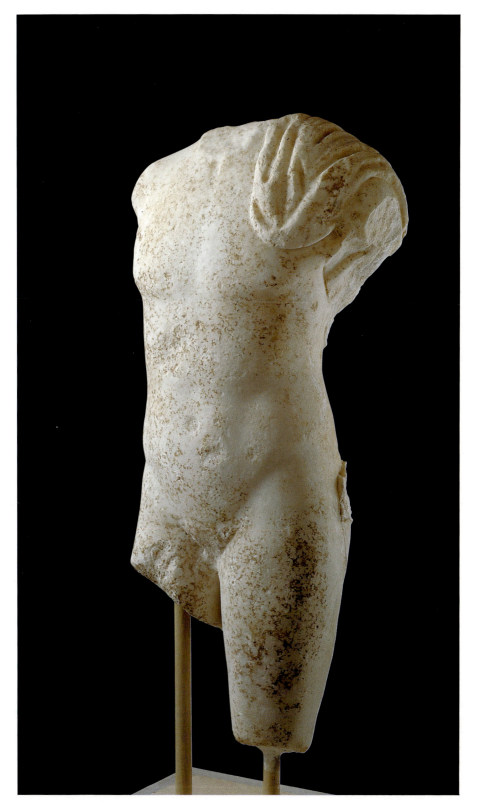

Fig. 94. Torso of a statue of a naked child, half-kneeling (A 260). Hellenistic period (?).

and, at the back right, the upper part of a torso of a dressed female figure (A 981); on the third shelf are displayed small votive slabs from the sanctuary of Eileithyia: at the left A 305-306 (fig. 90) and one with breasts A 307 (fig. 91), and other votive plaques with relief ears (A 697),at the right: (A 564) a relief stylized depiction of female pudenda, and (A 135) relief breasts a left foot wearing a sandal (A 173). On the floor beneath the case are large vases, mainly of the Hellenistic period, from the cemetery near the ancient harbour. Other finds in this room worth noting include : on the east wall, the torso of a naked youth with a himation thrown over his left shoulder (A 977) (fig. 93), part of a frieze with relief decoration of bucrania and floral scrolls (A 33) (fig. 97) high on the wall, the torso of a naked boy half-kneeling (A 260) (fig. 94), the head of a lion (A 423); on the south wall, grave reliefs of the Roman period: A 798, on which red paint from the decoration is still preserved and above it, on the wall, A 195 with a scene of a funeral banquet, A 1353 (below the window) from a sarcophagus and, next to the window, at the top, an inscribed stele with a pediment and a depiction of a little girl (A 764); beneath this stele is another, also inscribed (A 452), portraying a small naked child with a chlamys on its shoulder.

THE COURTYARD

Most of the antiquities in the courtyard, as we have seen, are grave monuments of various kinds from Parikia and the Parian countryside. Along the south side of the courtyard are sarcophagi in the shape of a human body, dating from the first half of the 5th c. BC, which are the only ones of their kind so far found in the Greek world (fig. 95). Similar sarcophagi have been found in Phoenicia, and they are regarded as a Phoenician type; their presence on Paros, however, gives rise to questions as to the workshop that made them (whether Phoenician or Parian), since Paros is known to have enjoyed relations with regions on the east coast of the Mediterranean, such as Phoenicia, and even further south, with Egypt. Testimony to the relations between Egypt and Paros is afforded by the presence of Egyptian offerings at the Delion (see p. 59, case 5) and conversely, by the discovery in Egypt of Parian drachmas dating from the late 6th and early 5th c. BC. together with coins of Thasos, a Parian colony. On the east side of the courtyard is an impressive group consisting of a Classical sarcophagus standing on a tall crepis in the shape of the Greek letter Π (A 1242, A 1246) of later date, which were found together at the beginning of the 1960s in the area of the large cemetery near the ancient harbour. Towards the north on this same side of the courtyard are five marble stelae with roughly-worked surfaces; on the front there is a dressed area at the top of the stele containing the inscription ΟΡΟΣ ΧΩΡΙΟ ΙΕΡΟ ΑΠΟΛΛΩΝΟΣ ΔΗΛΙΟ (boundary of the area sacred to Apollo Delios) (fig. 98). These stelae were found to the north-west of Parikia and the inscriptions on them are evidence that there were plots of land that belonged to the sanctuary of Delian Apollo.

In the north wall of the courtyard are five niches. The easternmost contains an enormous pithos with embossed and incised linear dec-

Fig. 95. Sarcophagus in the shape of a human body. First half of the 5th c. BC.

oration, typical of Cycladic pottery workshops of the 6th c. BC and found on similar vases. Architectural members are displayed next to the pithos. In the next niche there is an interesting headless statue (A 780) of a standing goddess, probably Artemis, wearing an Attic peplos, which is tied under the breast. A band crossing the back obliquely from the right shoulder holds the quiver (3rd-2nd c. BC). In the third niche is a larger than life size statue of a man wearing a himation, roughly contemporary with the statue of Artemis. (A 738 and A 868). To the right is part of a votive stele with a depiction of Artemis (A 192). The goddess wears a short chiton, has her legs astride, and in her raised right hand holds an object that is difficult to make out. Behind her at the right is a tree with a snake. Next to this is another relief (A 735) with Artemis, wearing a short chiton and himation. She is depicted frontally and behind her right shoulder wears the quiver, towards which she raises her right hand. To the left of her is an altar. At the back of the niche are displayed grave stelae, on one of which is depicted an enthroned woman with

Fig. 96. Sarcophagus of the Classical period (5th c. BC), set on a crepis of late Roman date (A 1242, A 1246).

Fig. 97. Part of a frieze decorated with bucrania and garlands (A 33). Late Hellenistic period (?).

Fig. 98. Marble stele inscribed ΟΡΟΣ ΧΩΡΙΟ ΑΠΟΛΛΩΝΟΣ ΔΗΛΙΟ (Boundary of the area sacred to Appolo Delios), from the area to the north-east of Parikia. Second half of the 5th c. BC.

a girl in front of her holding a small box (A 112). On the shelf in the fourth niche can be seen simas with water-spouts in the shape of lion's heads (4th-3rd c. BC), and at the bottom, a large part of a sarcophagus dating from late antiquity with a small relief scene. In the westernmost niche, the shelf contains grave reliefs with scenes of funeral banquets, and below them the front of a large sarcophagus with relief scenes and inscriptions. The type of these sarcophagi will be discussed below (see p. 88). On the west side of the courtyard are displayed architectural members, mainly parts of entablatures and triglyphs. There is also a large number of architectural members in the middle of the courtyard, which were reused as grave monuments and usually have relief scenes of funeral banquets; around the foot of the palm tree stand a large number of grave reliefs of different periods (5th-2nd c. BC) and types: stelai or simply bases, usually inscribed, marble cinerary urns with or without lids and with the name of the dead person frequently on the lid or below the rim of the vase. There are also some altars, one of them near the north side being a very fine large one decorated with bucrania and floral scrolls. Near this altar is displayed a statue consisting of two female torsoes attached at their backs (A 460). Each torso wears a peplos which is folded over and tied beneath the breast, while the bottom of the peplos is drawn up to the side. In the west part of the courtyard is displayed a large part of a mosaic floor with scenes from the labours

Fig. 99. The west part of the Museum courtyard, with a mosaic floor decorated with scenes from the labours of Herakles. 3rd c. AD.

Fig. 100. Mosaic floor with scenes from the labours of Herakles. From a gymnasium building. Detail. 3rd c. AD.

Fig. 101. Marble sarcophagus with a gabled lid and relief scenes set in square and rectangular recesses in the sides. 2nd-3rd c. AD.

of Herakles (figs 99, 100). It comes from a gymnasium building that was in use about AD 300 and occupied a site on which a Christian church was later built, which was in turn succeeded by the large Byzantine church of the Katapoliani. To the south of the mosaic, near the entrance to the Museum, is a scarcely worked marble stele which bears the inscription *ΟΡΟΣ ΠΟΛΕΩΣ* "city boundary" in three lines. Stelai of this type are known as ὅροι ("boundary markers") and were used to mark the boundaries of a city. This one was found in the place where it was made, in an ancient quarry at Lakki.

Outside the west size of the courtyard, along the whole of the west wall, is a stepped base bearing a number of marble sarcophagi, which are amongst the finest of their kind. These sarcophagi served as family tombs and are typical of Paros in the 2nd-3rd c. AD (fig. 101). On their sides, they had square or rectangular inset panels bearing relief scenes, most of which were in the type of the funeral banquet, with inscriptions accompanying the scenes around them. The lid was normally gabled, and had busts, probably of the heads of the family.

ABBREVIATIONS-BIBLIOGRAPHY

AA: Archäologischer Anzeiger
AM: Mitteilungen des Deutschen Archäologischen Instituts, Athenische Abteilung
BCH: Bulletin de Correspondance Hellénique
EAA: Enciclopedia dell'Arte Antica

D. Berranger, Recherches sur l'histoire et la prosopographie de Paros à l'époque archaïque, Clermont Ferrand, France 1992, with full previous bibliography.
EAA, Secondo Supplemento, IV, 1996, s.v. Paros [G. Gruben].
A. Kostoglou-Despoini, Προβλήματα παριανής πλαστικής, Thessaloniki 1989.
Eug. Lanzillota, Paro dall'età arcaica all'età ellenistica, Roma 1987, with the relevant bibliography at that time.
Eug. Lanzillota e Dem. Schilardi, Le Cicladi ed il Mondo Egeo, Roma, 19-21 Novembre 1992, Roma 1996.
An. Merky, Römische Grabreliefs und Sarkophage auf den Kykladen, Frankfurt am Main 1995.
O. Rubensohn, Paros I, AM 25 (1900), p. 341-372; Paros II, AM 26 (1901), p. 157-222; Paros III, AM 27 (1902), p. 189-238.
N. Zaphiropoulos, Αρχαϊκές κόρες της Πάρου, in Archaische und klassische griechische Plastik, Berlin 1986, p. 93 f.
Ph. Zaphiropoulou, Banquets funéraires sur des reliefs de Paros, BCH CXV (1991), p. 525 f.
Ph. Zaphiropoulou, Une nécropole à Paros, in Nécropoles et sociétés antiques, Cahiers du Centre Jean Bérard, XVIII, Naples 1994, p. 127 f.
Ph. Zaphiropoulou, Sepulcralia Varia Cycladica, Πρακτικά Α' Κυκλαδικού Συνεδρίου, Άνδρος, 5-9 Σεπτεμβρίου 1991, Επετηρίς Κυκλαδικών Μελετών, ΙΕ (1995), p. 228 f.